MYSTERIES

OF

PLANETS, STARS, AND GALAXIES

by Lela Nargi

CAPSTONE PRESS
a capstone imprint

Capstone Captivate is published by Capstone Press, an imprint of Capstone.
1710 Roe Crest Drive
North Mankato, Minnesota 56003
www.capstonepub.com

Library of Congress Cataloging-in-Publication Data is available on the Library of Congress website.
ISBN: 978-1-4966-8079-2 (library binding)
ISBN: 978-1-4966-8718-0 (paperback)
ISBN: 978-1-4966-8172-0 (eBook PDF)

Summary: Does life exist somewhere other than Earth? How many planets are outside our galaxy? What happens when stars crash into each other? Budding astronomers will learn all about planets, stars, and galaxies, from what's already known to what scientists are still hoping to find out.

Image Credits
Alamy: Pictorial Press Ltd, 9 (Top), Science History Images, 9 (Bottom); Getty Images: Hulton Archive/Stringer, 8; NASA, 9 (Middle), 21, Ames Research Center, 11; Newscom: Reuters/Mike Theiler, 26, Science Photo Library/Mark Garlick, 28, ZUMA Press/Keystone Pictures USA, 10; Science Source: European Southern Observatory, 27, Mikkel Juul Jensen, 22; Shutterstock: D1min, 25 (Top), Dotted Yeti, 20, meunierd, 7, Nasky, 6, 12, NikoNomad, Cover, PlusONE, 25 (Bottom), sdecoret, 5, Zack Frank, 17; Wikimedia: ESO/M. Kornmesser/Nick Risinger (skysurvey.org), 19, NASA, 16, NASA/IMAX, 15

Design Elements
Shutterstock: Anna Kutukova, Aygun Ali

Editorial Credits
Editor: Hank Musolf; Designer: Sara Radka; Media Researcher: Jo Miller; Production Specialist: Laura Manthe

All internet sites appearing in back matter were available and accurate when this book was sent to press.

Printed in the United States of America.
PA117

TABLE OF CONTENTS

Words in **bold** appear in the glossary.

CHAPTER 1

IS ANYBODY OUT THERE?

Isn't Earth a great planet? It is home to almost 9 million species of living things. It has tall mountains and deep oceans. For thousands of years we humans have wondered if that's all there is. Does life exist somewhere else? Where in space should we look?

STARS, PLANETS, GALAXIES PRIMER

Galaxies have different shapes. Elliptical galaxies look like stretched-out circles. They are made when small galaxies crash into each other. Spiral galaxies twirl from a bulge of stars in the middle. The Milky Way is a barred spiral galaxy with two swirling arms. It is one of 54 galaxies in the Local Group. Other galaxies are blobs or shaped like lentils.

We have looked for answers in different ways. We have pondered why our sun supports life here but not on planets like Jupiter. We have built rovers that have explored Mars. We have peered through telescopes at moons and stars. We have hunted through space. Is anyone out there?

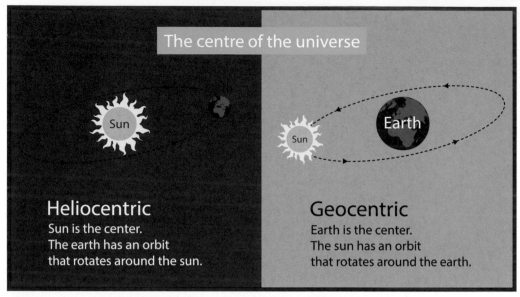

geocentric and heliocentric models of the solar system

(NOT) THE CENTER OF THE UNIVERSE

First, people on Earth had to learn a hard lesson.

Ancient Greeks counted eight "planets." These were Earth, Mercury, Venus, Mars, Jupiter, Saturn, the sun, and our moon. Astronomers thought they orbited Earth in a **geocentric** system.

A philosopher named Anaxagoras eventually figured out that the sun was a star. Then astronomer Aristarchus of Samos figured out that the planets revolve around the sun in a **heliocentric** system.

This idea didn't stick until the early 1500s, though. That's when Nicolaus Copernicus wrote that Mercury, Venus, Earth, Mars, Jupiter, and Saturn orbited the sun. This surprised and amazed people.

Nicolaus Copernicus

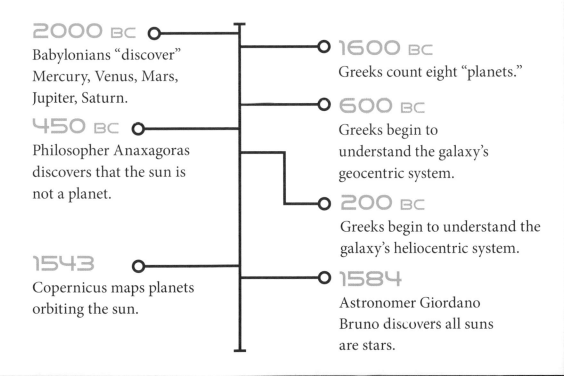

2000 BC
Babylonians "discover" Mercury, Venus, Mars, Jupiter, Saturn.

450 BC
Philosopher Anaxagoras discovers that the sun is not a planet.

1543
Copernicus maps planets orbiting the sun.

1600 BC
Greeks count eight "planets."

600 BC
Greeks begin to understand the galaxy's geocentric system.

200 BC
Greeks begin to understand the galaxy's heliocentric system.

1584
Astronomer Giordano Bruno discovers all suns are stars.

CHAPTER 2

BEYOND OUR SOLAR SYSTEM

People can see about 2,000 stars with our naked eyes. In 1610, Italian astronomer Galileo Galilei built a telescope and pointed it at the sky. Then people could see many more stars in our Milky Way galaxy.

Galileo Galilei

Later telescopes helped us find Uranus, Neptune, Pluto, and numerous moons orbiting the planets.

MYSTERY FACT

What shape is the universe? The universe could be shaped like a closed-off sphere, or something more flat that keeps spreading out. All scientists know for sure is that the universe is much larger than what we can see.

Edwin Hubble built another telescope in the 1920s. It showed us far out past our galaxy.

Suddenly the universe was huge! Some of the stars we thought we had been looking at? Some of them were actually galaxies. They held countless stars, and maybe even planets like ours.

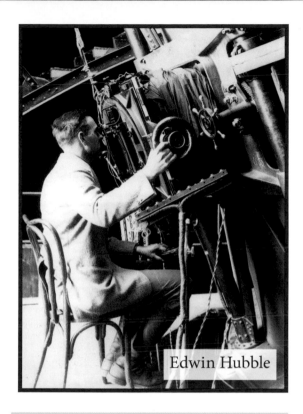

Edwin Hubble

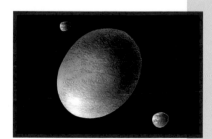

Haumea

Eris

CHANGING PLANETS

We didn't only think the moon and sun were planets in the past. We thought Pluto and Ceres were, too. They are small space objects and have weak gravity. They were renamed dwarf planets in 2006. We have named three other dwarf planets in our solar system. They are Haumea, Eris, and Makemake.

A CLOSER LOOK

How do you study a huge and crowded universe? You start small. You start with a solar system that's billions of miles wide.

Astronomers started to send probes into our solar system in the 1960s. They took pictures. They measured heat and gases.

We learned that Jupiter is mostly liquid. Mars is dusty and dotted with inactive volcanoes. The surface of Mercury is like the Moon. The atmosphere of Venus has oxygen.

Mariner 9 was sent by NASA to explore Mars.

Pioneer 10 was the first spacecraft to explore Jupiter.

CHAPTER 3

WHAT LIFE NEEDS

Is there life on these planets? Was there life there once upon a time? **Astrobiologists** look for clues.

Life needs a perfect dose of light and energy. A just-right body orbits a star at just the right distance. This is called a **"Goldilocks Zone."**

HABITABLE ZONE OF THE SOLAR SYSTEM

Venus's atmosphere is nice and thick. But its surface is too hot. Life needs nutrients. Mars, Venus, Saturn's moon, Titan, and Jupiter's moon, Io, have those. Life needs water. Mars used to have surface water. It still has ice and liquid water below its surface.

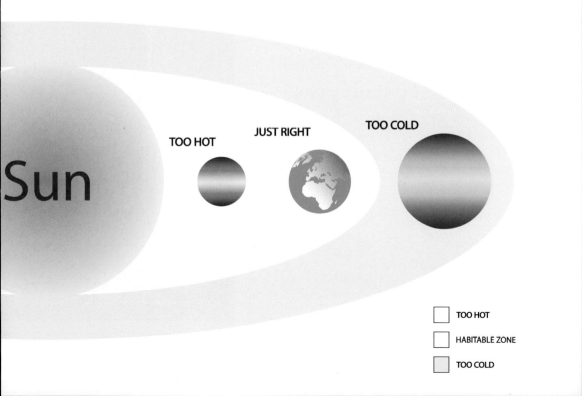

Sun

TOO HOT

JUST RIGHT

TOO COLD

TOO HOT

HABITABLE ZONE

TOO COLD

BEYOND OUR GALAXY

NASA sent the Hubble Space Telescope deep into space in 1990. The universe as we knew it changed forever. We saw stars being born and dying. We saw that there could be trillions of galaxies in our universe.

Shortly after its launch, scientists noticed that images from the telescope were returning blurry. They realized the telescope wasn't working correctly. Two teams of astronauts went into space to fix it. Afterwards, the pictures came in clearly.

The Hubble Space Telescope was deployed into space on April 24, 1990.

CHAPTER 4

WHERE IS EVERYONE?

How can we search all these galaxies for **extraterrestrial** life? One way is to listen for it. *SETI* stands for the "search for extraterrestrial intelligence." SETI researchers started to point radio telescopes at space in 1959. They have been trying to hear signals ever since.

Another way is to send our own signals. We hope aliens hear or see us. We sent *Pioneer 10* toward the edge of the universe in 1972. It is still out in space.

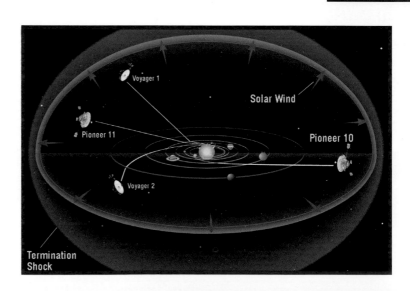

Spacecraft that are on trajectories to leave the solar system

The Very Large Array has 27 active antennas.

We sent radio signals to a star cluster called M13 in 1974. It is 21,000 light-years away.

We sent *Voyager 1* and *2* toward the other end of the universe in 1977. They are still out there, too. They are carrying discs of music, words, and photos.

THE DRAKE EFFECT

American mathematician Frank Drake thought there might be up to 1 billion intelligent civilizations in the Milky Way.

THE SOLAR SYSTEM IS NOT AS SPECIAL AS WE THOUGHT

By 1990, we had found some planets outside our solar system. Some wandered alone. Some hung out near dense stars called **pulsars**.

In 1995, two Swiss astronomers discovered Dimidium. It was 50 million light-years away. It orbited Helvetios, a star like our sun. Our solar system wasn't the only solar system.

Dimidium shocked scientists. It is so close to Helvetios that it has a four-day orbit. Earth's is 365 days. Dimidium's surface is 2,372 degrees Fahrenheit (1,300 degrees Celsius). That is the melting point of cast iron. There is no life on Dimidium!

Before finding Dimidium, scientists thought Dimidium-sized planets had to form far away from their stars.

MYSTERY FACT

Dimidium is a gas giant like our biggest planet, Jupiter. It's also hot. It's called a **hot Jupiter**.

51 Pegasi B is another name for Dimidium.

Scientists are also searching for exomoons, which are moons that orbit exoplanets.

CHAPTER 5

GOING EXTRASOLAR

After finding Dimidium, scientists started hunting for more **exoplanets** orbiting other stars. That was a job for the Kepler space telescope. It started looking at 150,000 stars close to Earth in 2009. Imagine holding your hand up toward the stars at night. The amount of sky it covers is the tiny piece of space Kepler studied. Kepler ran out of fuel in 2018. It had found 2,681 exoplanets by then. We have counted 4,043 exoplanets so far.

Some exoplanets are gas giants like Jupiter and Dimidium. Some are like hot super-Earths. They are Earth-sized but very near their stars. Some are ice giants like Uranus and Neptune. They have layers. Hydrogen and helium are on the outside. Water and ammonia slush are in the middle.

EXOPLANETS

Some exoplanets have 1-million-year orbits. About 7 of 1,000 exoplanets are **circumbinary**. That means they orbit two stars. They are also called Tatooine planets. That's the name of Luke Skywalker's planet in *Star Wars*. Some worlds circle three, four, five, six, even seven stars!

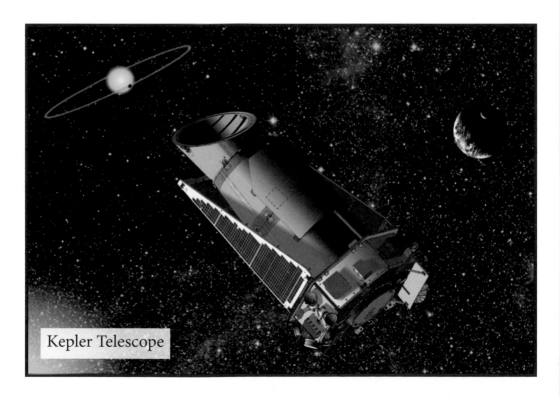

Kepler Telescope

Gamma Cephei

Capella

Castor   Aldebaran

Upsilon Andromeda

HD

47 U Majoris

Pollux

GJ 176

55 Cancri

V.

Zosma   GJ 436

Sun

Altair

Tau Ceti

83 Leonis

Denebola   Sirius

GJ 876

HD 69830

Alpha Centauri   GJ 581

GJ 1214

GJ 317

61 Virginis

HD 40307

HD 10647

Beta Pictoris

Epsilon Reticuli

Mu A

Tau Centauri   HD 113538

eramin

354

51 Pegasi

GJ 777

HD 189733

GJ 849

HD 217107

Rasalhaque

alhaut

GJ 785

Solar neighborhood

THE GOLDILOCKS ZONE: JUST RIGHT

There are at least 100 billion stars in our galaxy. Almost every one has at least one planet circling it. We've found 3,000 planetary systems so far. That number gets bigger all the time. One-quarter of planets are the size of Earth. They orbit in a Goldilocks Zone where it's not too hot and not too cold.

That means there are 25 billion worlds where life could exist just in the Milky Way. Life could be microscopic. Life could be like the **extremophiles** we have on Earth. They live in very hot or very cold places. Life could be like nothing we have seen.

CHAPTER 6

A VAST UNIVERSE

Why haven't we found life in space yet? Perhaps it's because the universe is vast.

Scientists compare it to a (very big) ocean. So far, we've only looked for alien life in the amount of water that could fill a hot tub. This might sound like a very small space, but it's big progress. In 2010, we'd only searched a drinking glass amount of water.

We also have a limited number of spacecraft and tools to aid our search. We have sent 300 spacecraft out of Earth's orbit.

Saturn

Neptune

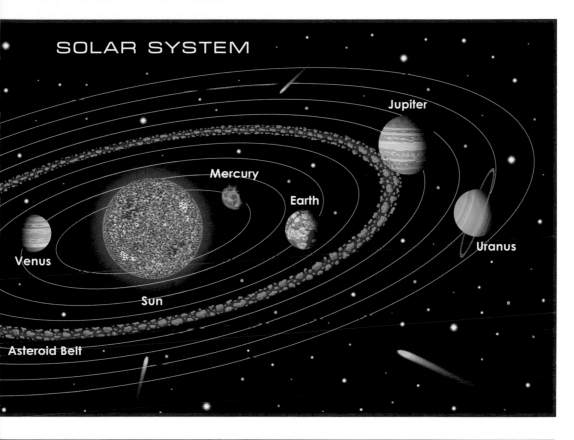

SOLAR SYSTEM

Jupiter

Mercury

Earth

Uranus

Venus

Sun

Asteroid Belt

OTHER WAYS OF SEEING

We have other tools to help us hunt for life. Scientists peer through very strong telescopes here on Earth. These can block out light from bright stars and our atmosphere.

This makes it easier to see **biosignatures**. They might be gases such as oxygen, methane, ozone, and carbon dioxide. Every living thing we know of emits gases. Another biosignature would be the green chlorophyll in plants.

Astronomer Nikole Lewis

We are also looking for **technosignatures**. These are signs of technology and life advanced enough to build it. The signs could be radio waves, laser waves, or lots of pollution.

La Silla Observatory

Artwork of alien plants on a hospitable foreign world

WHERE DO WE GO FROM HERE?

Some things we learn make the hunt for aliens seem hopeless. Maybe only 10 percent of galaxies can hold life. That is because of star blasts called gamma ray bursts. They wipe out any life bigger than a tiny microbe.

Sometimes it seems like we are on the verge of a big breakthrough. Mars has a lake of water under its surface. Sure, it's super cold and super salty. But it may have held life once. Scientists want to study Mars more closely.

There's an exoplanet called LTT 1445Ab in a three-star system 22.5 light-years away. It has an atmosphere. There could be life there now. And soon, we'll send a lander to Jupiter's moon, Europa. It's got a whole ocean of water that maybe holds nutrients. Who knows what we will find next!

GLOSSARY

astrobiologist (AS-truh-by-ah-luh-jist)—a scientist who studies whether there's life off Earth, often by studying how life on Earth works

biosignature (BY-oh-sig-nuh-chur)—any sign of past or present life

circumbinary (suhr-kuhm-BY-nayr-ee)—planet that orbits two stars

exoplanet (EK-soh-plan-it)—planet that orbits a star outside of the solar system

extraterrestrial (ek-struh-tuh-RESS-tree-uhl)—a life form that comes from outer space

extremophile (ek-STREEM-oh-fy-uhl)—something that lives in extreme conditions

geocentric (GEE-oh-sen-trik)—with Earth (*geo*) at the center

Goldilocks Zone (gohl-DEE-loks ZOHN)—a place that's not too hot or too cold for an Earth-like planet to exist

heliocentric (HEEL-ee-oh-sehn-trik)—with the sun at the center

hot Jupiter (HOT JOO-pih-tuhr)—an exoplanet that's like Jupiter, only much closer to its star

pulsar (PUHL-sahr)—a very dense star made up of the center of a burst star

technosignature (tek-NO-sig-nuh-chuhr)—any sign of technology

READ MORE

Simon, Seymour. *Exoplanets.* New York: HarperCollins, 2018.

Sparrow, Giles. *Universe.* New York: DK Publishing, 2018.

Stewart, Melissa. *Out of This World Jokes About the Solar System.* Berkeley Heights, NJ: Enslow Elementary, 2012.

INTERNET SITES

NASA Kids Club
nasa.gov/kidsclub/index.html

NASA Science Space Place
spaceplace.nasa.gov/

Science News for Students: Space
sciencenewsforstudents.org/topic/space-0

INDEX